POCKET STUDY SKILLS

Series Editor: **Kate Williams**,
Oxford Brookes University, UK
Illustrations by Sallie Godwin

Pocket Study Skills
Series Standing Order
ISBN 978-0230-21605-1
(outside North America only)

For the time-pushed student, the *Pocket Study Skills* pack a lot of advice into a little book. Each guide focuses on a single crucial aspect of study, giving you step-by-step guidance, handy tips and clear advice on how to approach the important areas which will continually be at the core of your studies.

Published

14 Days to Exam Success

Blogs, Wikis, Podcasts and More

Brilliant Writing Tips for Students

Completing Your PhD

Doing Research

Getting Critical (2nd edn)

Planning Your Dissertation

Planning Your Essay (2nd edn)

Planning Your PhD

Posters and Presentations

Reading and Making Notes (2nd edn)

Referencing and Understanding Plagiarism

Reflective Writing

Report Writing

Science Study Skills

Studying with Dyslexia

Success in Groupwork

Time Management

Writing for University

POSTERS & PRESENTATIONS

POCKET STUDY SKILLS

Emily Bethell and
Clare Milsom

BLOOMSBURY ACADEMIC
LONDON • NEW YORK • OXFORD • NEW DELHI • SYDNEY

BLOOMSBURY ACADEMIC
Bloomsbury Publishing Plc
50 Bedford Square, London, WC1B 3DP, UK
1385 Broadway, New York, NY 10018, USA
29 Earlsfort Terrace, Dublin 2, Ireland

BLOOMSBURY, BLOOMSBURY ACADEMIC and the Diana logo
are trademarks of Bloomsbury Publishing Plc

First published by RED GLOBE PRESS, 2014
Reprinted by Bloomsbury Academic, 2024

ISBN: PB: 978-1-1373-5708-3
ePDF: 978-1-1373-5709-0

To find out more about our authors and books visit www.bloomsbury.com and sign up for our newsletters.

Contents

About the authors

Dr Emily Bethell is a Senior Lecturer in Primate Behaviour at Liverpool John Moores University, UK where she assesses student posters and presentations in the biological and psychological sciences. Emily is a co-author on the *Planning* and *Completing Your PhD* books in the Palgrave Pocket Study Skills series.

Dr Clare Milsom is Assistant Academic Registrar at Liverpool John Moores University. Clare has over 20 years' experience of teaching and assessing undergraduate and postgraduate students and uses poster and presentation assessment in her modules. She has written a key undergraduate text for geology students and she currently runs the PGCertLTHE teaching course for university staff.

Both authors have won prizes for their presentations.

Acknowledgements

Thank you to the following people: Kate Williams, Suzannah Burywood, Caroline Richards, Bryony Ross and all the 'behind the scenes' staff at Palgrave Macmillan for their guidance, hard work and tolerance throughout the writing, editorial and print processes; Sallie Godwin for her illustrations; and the anonymous reviewers for their invaluable feedback. For real life examples of student posters and presentations and staff teaching materials and feedback we thank: Adam Papworth, Anne-Marie Adams, Kevin Arbuckle, Mandy Holmes, Evan MacLean, Elizabeth Brannon, Maria Forde, Nicola Koyama, Marcia Worrell, Hazel Nichols, Charlotte Buckley, Katie Garland, Sarah Vick, Tara Mandalaywala, Andy Tattersall, Terry Donovan, Grace Hillary, Menna Jones, Mel Hills and Catherine Groves. Finally, we thank all our fantastic students who make teaching this stuff so rewarding.

Introduction

Background

How to communicate ideas effectively is a central skill taught at university, whatever your level of study, degree subject or country. Posters and oral presentations are two ways of communicating ideas in a highly visual, creative and direct way.

Posters and presentation assessments at university are important for improving your:

- visual and oral communication skills
- ability to distil and express your ideas clearly
- flexibility and effectiveness in communicating with a wide range of audiences
- employability: communication skills are essential whatever your career aspirations.

Posters and presentation assignments can be the most fun and rewarding, yet they are also the assignments that students get most anxious about. This book will show you what is involved and explain how to prepare well to maximise your potential.

How we planned the book

We planned this book to be a user-friendly guide to working on poster and presentation assignments at university. Using a series of workshops, we take you step by step through four key stages, thinking, planning, doing, and reflecting, so you can improve.

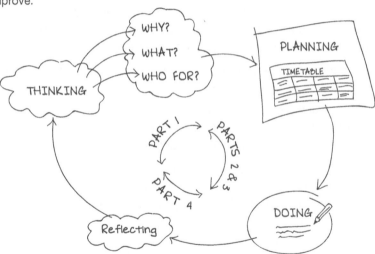

About this book

Part 1 Getting started tells you what your university tutors want and how to get good marks. A series of workshops will develop your skills in the core processes (**thinking** and **planning**) required to start making brilliant posters and presentations.

Part 2 is about **'doing' posters** and shows how to apply the core thinking and planning processes covered in Part 1 to make great posters.

Part 3 is about **'doing' presentations** and shows how to think and plan to make excellent presentations.

Part 4 is about **reflecting to improve** and shows how to interpret feedback and do even better next time. There are tips to help you stand out and ideas for how these skills will be useful in your life after university.

1 — Getting strategic (why, what, who)

Be strategic and use the 6 Ps:

Proper Planning and Preparation
Prevent Poor Performance

Ninety per cent of your coursework is planning and preparation. Be strategic. Plan and prepare well.

WHY

Why have you been asked to produce a poster or presentation? You are given coursework so you can demonstrate that you have met specific **learning outcomes**. You can find these in the **course handbook** or module proforma.

1st year Ecology module:

After completing the module, you should be able to demonstrate the following **learning outcomes**:

1 Identify common behaviours in selected species and explain their purpose.

2 Recognise the influence of the environment on the distribution and abundance of organisms.

Assessments and their learning outcomes

Assessment	Learning outcome	What this means for you ...
Poster	1	Your poster will show the **relationship between behaviour and purpose** in selected species, using minimal text, good visuals and clear sections and headings.
Group presentation	2	You should take it in turns to talk about the **influence** of the **environment** on the **distribution** and **abundance** of **organisms**. Each student should talk about a different environmental factor, or group of organisms. Slides should be coordinated (font, colour) with limited text and good pictures. Be prepared to answer questions after.

Adapted from 1st year Natural Sciences course, LJMU

3rd year Engineering module:

1. Demonstrate the ability to conceive, plan and execute a substantial design project.
2. Critically review published research relevant to the project.
3. Work effectively in a team.
4. Demonstrate effective verbal communication skills.

Assessments and their learning outcomes

Assessment	Learning outcome	What this means for you ...
Poster (with supporting portfolio)	1, 3	You should **coordinate with group members** to produce a poster (with accompanying portfolio) that visually and succinctly summarises the **conception, planning and execution stages** of a **substantial design project**.
Individual presentation	1, 2, 4	You will discuss, with visual aids, the **conception, planning and execution** of your **design project** supported by thorough **research and evaluation of an established body of relevant knowledge**. You will also be assessed on your **verbal presentation skills**. Materials and delivery should be of a professional standard. Be ready to answer challenging questions.

Adapted from 3rd year Engineering course, LJMU

Summative assessment: measures your achievement
Formative assessment: tells you how to improve

Both may be marked but only summative assessments count towards your final mark. Read and act on feedback on both types of assessment: this will help you to improve.

 The module handbook is a valuable tool for understanding how university staff planned the course, and what you need to do to excel.

Workshop 1: WHY

→ Gather materials: course handbook, online resources, lecture notes, handouts.
→ Identify the learning outcomes for your assignment.

The learning outcomes for this assignment are:

First learning outcome: ....

What I need to do: ....

Second learning outcome: ....

What I need to do: ....

WHAT

What you are expected to do is given in the **assignment guidelines** and **assessment criteria** for your poster or presentation. Your mark will reflect how well you follow the guidelines, according to the criteria. This is an opportunity to show you can produce a product that meets someone else's specified standards: 'This is what you asked me to do … here it is (and I did it well) ☺.' Being able to follow instructions and deliver a product, or fulfil a client brief, will make you highly employable when you graduate.

First, get the academic content right – the processes that underlie your coursework assignments are largely the same; it is just the *form of delivery* that differs. A good-looking poster, or a confidently delivered oral presentation, will get a low mark if the content is not up to scratch! So do your research.

It's all part of the process …

The assignment guidelines contain information ('process' or 'instruction' words) about what is expected of you and how you should go about researching the content. If you are instructed to 'evaluate' a topic, make sure you present an appraisal of that topic and not just a description. See *Getting Critical* in this series for a more in-depth discussion of process words.

Analyse: break down into component parts

Compare: examine similarities and **Contrast:** examine differences

Critique: weigh up evidence for and against different arguments and present your own subjective opinion

Define: give clear and concise meanings, including limitations

Describe: state the identifying characteristics

Discuss: examine issues and debates on a subject, present different cases, including the pros and cons of each and your own interesting response to them

Evaluate: weigh up evidence for and against different arguments with objective comment on their relative value

Explain: state the how or why of an issue

Illustrate: give examples, case studies, figures or diagrams that support your argument or help clarify issues being discussed

Interpret: translate or solve a problem giving an answer based on a clear line of reasoning

Justify: present evidence for your decisions/conclusions/interpretations

Outline: state all of the main points, common themes and major differences; avoid small details

Review: identify the major themes or existing range of knowledge in a subject area; also requires you to **critically evaluate*** the material reviewed

*see definitions for both critique and evaluate

'Describe the main types of business model, giving an example for each'

Make a list of the main business models from your course notes or core readings (e.g. course textbook), writing a description and giving clear examples.

'Evaluate the evidence for climate change'

Identify arguments - course materials, literature search (use library search engines; web of knowledge; Google Scholar). Weigh up the evidence for and against each argument. Which studies/arguments are most convincing and why?

> TOP TIP
> *Evidence may be supportive of an argument, but not conclusive. There may be grey areas or caveats such as 'our study provides evidence that ... however ... we need more data ...'. Discussing the gaps and uncertainties in a research area is exactly the kind of detail that your assessors will be impressed by. Recent review papers and meta-analyses* provide useful summaries of the current state of knowledge and strength of opinions.*

A **review paper** discusses the findings from a large number of papers (and different research groups) and summarises the general themes and future directions. A **meta-analysis paper** presents an analysis of the data from lots of studies conducted by different research groups at different times.

Workshop 2: Using the assignment guidelines – process words

→ Write down the key process words in the **assignment guidelines**.
→ Write what each word means, and what you need to do to achieve it (start with process words given in the assignment title).
→ Reread the assignment title. Make sure you answer *all of the question*.

Process word 1: Evaluate …

This means I need to … *weigh up evidence for and against different arguments with objective comment on their relative value …*

I will do this by … *finding journal articles on the topic (especially recent review papers or meta-analyses), identifying the main arguments and objectively assessing their relative merit: which arguments are most widely supported by researchers?; published in the best journals?; sample size and methodological issues. I will use my study skills module notes, Getting Critical in this series, and sign up for the library course on literature reviews.*

> **Your process word 1**: ....
>
> This means I need to: ....
>
> ....
>
> I will do this by: ....
>
> ....

Now go and research your topic! Use your notes from Workshops 1 and 2 to keep you on track.

Content with the content?

Have you ever received feedback saying *You have not answered the question*? Before you write anything (but after you have done your research!), know what it is you want to say.

Your message should be:

▶ clear, concise and answer the question
▶ interesting and informative
▶ attractive and attention grabbing.

Workshop 3: Using the assignment guidelines – message and content

→ Take your literature search notes, notes from Workshops 1 and 2 and a sheet of paper.

→ Write *'My message is ...'* in the centre of the sheet.

→ Write down all the keywords that relate to your assignment topic.

→ Circle the KEY words that relate to the PRIMARY MESSAGE you want to convey – these should appear in the main text/words and title.

→ Remove words that are *not* directly related to your primary message – these should *not* appear in your title or main text (but may be mentioned in the discussion or during a question session as future directions or wider implications).

→ Store this in your work folder and refer to it regularly to keep on track!

My message is:

....

....

....

....

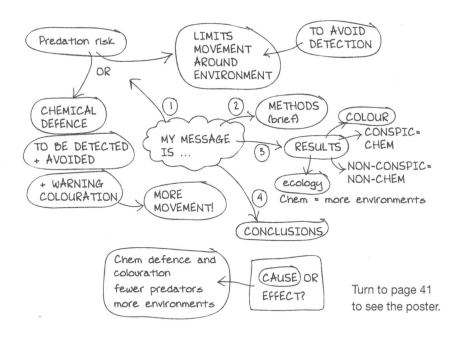

Predation risk

CHEMICAL DEFENCE

TO BE DETECTED + AVOIDED

+ WARNING COLOURATION

MORE MOVEMENT!

OR

LIMITS MOVEMENT AROUND ENVIRONMENT

TO AVOID DETECTION

① MY MESSAGE IS ...

② METHODS (brief)

③ RESULTS

COLOUR

CONSPIC = CHEM

NON-CONSPIC = NON-CHEM

ecology

Chem = more environments

④ CONCLUSIONS

Chem defence and colouration
fewer predators
more environments

CAUSE OR EFFECT?

Turn to page 41 to see the poster.

Assessment criteria

Research shows that students who spend time considering the assessment criteria prior to starting a piece of work get significantly higher marks than students who do not (Rust, Price and O'Donovan 2003).

Class/grade	Assignments/essays
First class work	
90–100%	Outstanding work showing creative ability. Excellent critical evaluation of all issues with <u>development of original material</u>. Extensive reading used to direct arguments. Outstanding level of intellectual work.
80–90%	Very high quality work showing clear understanding of the subject matter. Good critical evaluation covering all issues. Reading used to direct arguments. Very high level of intellectual work.

Terms like 'creative ability' and 'originality' indicate you have developed your own well-informed ideas, can communicate them well and have something to contribute to the field. These qualities will set you apart as an outstanding student.

Class/grade	Assignments/essays
First class work	
70–80%	High quality work showing strong grasp of subject matter. Some critical evaluation. Arguments well formulated and sustained. Consideration of all dominant issues. Selective use of relevant <u>literature</u>.
Satisfactory work	
60–70%	Solid work showing competent understanding of subject matter. <u>Limited critical evaluation</u>. Arguments developed and supported with relevant literature. Appreciation of main issues with referencing. <u>Well prepared and presented material</u>. Writing coherent.
50–60%	Adequate work but lacking depth and breadth. <u>Descriptive</u> approach. Referencing unfocused. Competent writing.

At first class level, focus is on content. Your writing and presentation should already be of a high standard. You may be able to attend writing workshops for free at your university for help with this.

The reason many students gain a high second class mark rather than a first class mark is due to a lack of critical evaluation. Again – check out extra support to develop this skill

These are essential for a first class mark. Good preparation and presentation can improve your mark.

Suggests lack of critical evaluation. Arguments may be presented but are not fully developed. If you make a statement, be sure to follow it up with evidence.

From here to 'outstanding'

Take a look at these example assignments. What could you do to attain first-class criteria such as 'outstanding'?

Assignment	Good enough to pass	What can I do to be 'outstanding'?
'Describe the main types of business model, giving an example for each' (1st year, Business Studies)	List and describe examples given in course materials.	Make sure you describe *all* the relevant models you were given on the course.
		Present the information in a way that demonstrates your deeper understanding of the links or relationships between the different models. For example, group the models according to common themes, list them in chronological order, or distinguish currently favoured models from the less popular.
		Give examples from extra reading in addition to those listed in the course materials, or from your own experience.

Assignment	Good enough to pass	What can I do to be 'outstanding'?
'Evaluate the evidence for climate change' (3rd year, Environmental Sciences)	Present the arguments given in the course materials. Support with evidence from the key readings.	Give examples from extra reading, especially from very recent articles. Identify latest developments in the field, new directions for research, current controversies. Comment on the quality of the science (sample size, rigour of methods, how widely cited are papers or their authors). Are there problems with some methods or conclusions? Are there wider implications (e.g. for environmental policy)? (These may only need brief mention.)

In Parts 2 and 3 we present more specific, real-life examples of assessment criteria that are used for undergraduate posters and presentations.

Pay particular attention if you tend to avoid tackling criteria that are harder to grasp (such as 'high standard of critical evaluation', 'excellent analytical approach'). You are not alone (Rust, Price and O'Donovan 2003), but it will affect your final mark if you do not take time to think about what you are being asked to do. If you are still unsure about the meaning of some assessment criteria, take another look at the process words on p. 6.

Workshop 4: WHAT

Locate the **assessment criteria** for a first-class grade (aim high!).

The assessment criteria my tutor will use to assess that I have achieved the learning outcomes to a first-class standard are:

Criterion 1: *excellent use of visuals that clearly support the main argument being presented.* To achieve this I need to: *use high quality images, learn to use graphics software to create professional looking graphs containing all the correct elements* (see Chapters 7 and 11).

Criterion 2: *at least six peer-reviewed journal articles cited and referenced correctly.* To achieve this I need to: *do a thorough literature search to find the main researchers in the field and find key papers; identify which six present the best coverage of current knowledge; refer to my course notes on how to cite and reference papers.*

Your criterion 1: ....

To achieve this I need to: ....

....

Your criterion 2: ....

To achieve this I need to: ....

....

WHO

Who you will produce your poster or presentation for is your tutor: the person who will mark your work. This is the person who has told you which learning outcomes they want you to demonstrate, and what assessment criteria they will use to assess your learning. This is the person you need to keep happy!

The assignment guidelines may state a second, 'imagined' audience for your work in 'the real world'. When marking your work, the marker will read your poster or listen to your presentation as if they were not just your university tutor but also a member of the imagined audience.

WHO

Example imagined audience	How should you pitch to the imagined audience?
Customer to buy your product	Good clear sales pitch. What does the product do/offer? What problems does it solve? Clear, attractive, professional presentation of information.
Members of public	Grab attention with good graphics and a clear message (people are busy or might not speak your language).
Healthcare professionals	Your audience is professional, with expert knowledge but limited time. Images must be clear. Text/words must be concise and informative.
'Expert' academic audience	Make implications of your study for furthering knowledge clear. This audience wants depth and detail.

Workshop 5: WHO

Identify the **imagined** and **real** audience for your work. These may be given explicitly in the assignment details, or may be implicit. If in doubt, check with your tutor.

The assessment criteria my tutor will use to assess that I have achieved the learning outcomes to a first-class standard are:

Imagined audience: ....

I need to pitch to this audience in the following way:

....

....

Real audience (tutor): ....

I need to demonstrate that I have: *followed the assignment guidelines and meet the*

assessment criteria ....

....

2 Planning (how, when, where)

Here we discuss the core elements involved in planning presentations and posters. We discuss the differences in Parts 2 and 3.

Plan how to do it

Get organised. Which resources do you need to *do* the processes you have identified during your strategic thinking workshops (WS 1–5)? Sign up early for free study skills courses at your university (e.g. to use specialist software such as PowerPoint), additional support (e.g. to overcome anxiety about public speaking) or to access equipment and specialist resources (e.g. studio, laboratory space, computers, cameras).

If you are working in a group it can be difficult to find times when everyone can meet. Materials need to be sent around for agreement, and you may have to wait for feedback from other students. This means group work may take longer than when working alone. See pp. 24-6 for more tips on managing group work, as well as links to useful planning resources.

Plan when to do it

1 **Plan the big picture.** Write *all* your deadlines on a year planner. Add other commitments such as lectures, work shifts and holidays. Use colour coding to distinguish university work from employment and holiday time. This will give you an overview of when you have time available to do your coursework.

2 **Plan the next milestone.** Use this book to identify the key milestones for your coursework: gathering materials, doing your research (reading), writing drafts (are there feedback deadlines on drafts?), editing, printing, presenting.

3 **Plan the week ahead.** Write weekly and daily TO DO lists – and stick to them!

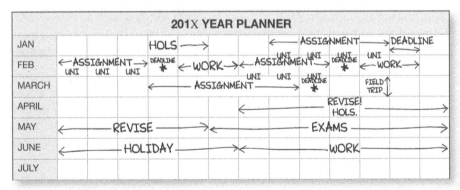

201X YEAR PLANNER

You will be given specific instructions about an assignment some weeks before the deadline. This is to give you time to *think*, *plan* and *do* your work. Little and often is the key. And start early. For more on how to plan your time, see *Time Management* in this series.

Plan where to do it

Find where you work best and make a point of working there. There may be different locations for the thinking, planning, reading, writing, editing and rehearsing components of your coursework. If you are working in a group, you may find meeting up in a location away from the university (city library, café) keeps things exciting.

BREAKING NEWS: You may hand work in BEFORE the deadline!!! Your marker will be impressed with your organisation skills.

The changing shape of university assignments

Your assignments will change in their emphasis and difficulty as you progress through your degree.

In your first year of study your assignments will be about making sure all students (from a wide range of backgrounds) have the same foundation knowledge. There will be lots of instruction, with a focus on training you in the skills you will be assessed on in the final years.

Be aware of this change in emphasis from tutor-guided training towards independent demonstration of learning.

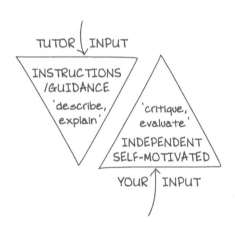

Plan in advance. Knowing what is expected of you in the final year (e.g. evaluative and analytical skills; see p. 6 'process words') will help you to understand what skills you are developing in the first and second years.

- In the *first year* you will learn basic skills and key principles.
- In the *second year* you will extend this knowledge and start developing your critical evaluation skills.
- In the *final year* you will be assessed on how well you have developed these skills. This is why many degree programmes give more marks for the final years.

Collect information for your assignments as you go. You can start as soon as you begin a course. Create a folder for each piece of coursework and save any images, notes, additional materials and useful links to websites in it. When you come to work on your assignment you will suddenly have a wealth of highly relevant information at your fingertips.

Group work

Group work is an integral part of your studies and of working life. It leads to deeper learning as you talk through areas of understanding and misunderstanding with other students, and employers value team communication skills. Being able to give examples of when and how you worked in a team will impress interviewers (especially if you can demonstrate your ability to reflect on what worked, what didn't, and how you would go about improving performance in the future). It is likely that working effectively in a group is one of your learning outcomes: take a look.

There are good reasons why posters and presentations are often done in a group:

- You will discuss issues with other students at a deeper level than usual, which will improve your understanding of the material and improve your verbal skills.
- Groups offer support, especially useful if you are nervous or struggling with the material.
- Group work builds social relationships within the class as a whole.
- Staff can see how the group functions as a unit, identify who put in effort and test who understands the material.

Success in Groupwork in this series covers this topic more fully. Here are a few pointers.

How to work in a group

1 **Dare to be different**. The most effective teams are diverse. People from different backgrounds increase scope for creative and original thought.

2 **Become a 'team'**. Get to know each other in the first meeting. Develop a supportive approach. Smile, ask questions, listen, take notes. By the end of the first meeting you should know everyone's names, how to contact them, when you will next meet and what everyone needs to do before the next meeting.

3 **Organise** yourselves and **share** the workload evenly.

4 An effective team **works to individuals' strengths**.

5 **Communicate**. Meet regularly to discuss the project. Also, meet at least once to review how the group roles and agreed practices are working out.

For planning and communicating with your team, use freely available online resources to:

▶ *organise meetings*: for example, Google Calendar: www.google.com/calendar and Doodle: www.doodle.com

▶ *share materials*: try Dropbox: www.dropbox.com

▶ *communicate*: social media such as Facebook and Twitter may provide an easier interface to communicate with the group than emails. Check what people use.

Always allow extra time for other group members to read communications and feedback.

Set deadlines and milestones at the start of the assignment so everyone is clear what they need to do and when.

Be flexible and sensitive to how other students work and any limitations they may have on their time (e.g. childcare and work shifts).

Are you a plant?

For a more in-depth look at how to work effectively in a team (and to find out if you are 'a plant') take a look at Belbin's team roles: www.belbin.com. This is a good system for understanding individuals' strengths and 'allowable weaknesses'. Doing the Belbin assessment together may be a good team-building exercise, as well as helping to identify individual strengths and assign team roles.

Potential problems and how to deal with them

Managing nerves

Having to talk in public, answer questions from your tutor, be assessed on your performance, meet and get to know strangers, deal with uncooperative group mates … these are all potentially anxiety-inducing situations. That is natural and will not change. What *can* change, however, is your ability to manage and cope with such situations.

- Learn to identify events and situations that make you anxious or nervous.
- Recognise that anxiety is a natural response to challenge: anxious situations are an opportunity to improve your personal resilience and develop new interpersonal skills.
- Practise techniques to reduce anxiety:
  - calm yourself with deep breathing or yoga
  - exercise regularly to release tension and enhance mood
  - eat a healthy balanced diet.
- Avoid unnecessary anxiety triggers:
  - recognise that alcohol and smoking can increase feelings of anxiety
  - avoid food and drink that contain stimulants such as caffeine, certain E-numbers and high sugar concentrations.

The best way to deal with nerves is to prepare well and practise, practise, practise.

If your nerves are so severe that you feel unable to overcome them, you should consider consulting a student welfare officer or your doctor. They will direct you to resources to help you manage your nerves.

The free-rider problem

Teaching staff are expert at identifying who has contributed to the team effort. If you feel members of the team are not pulling their weight, the coordinator will be able to feed this back to the assessor. The remaining team members should still do their best to create a good piece of work. The ability to step in to cover others when they can't or won't do their job is another professional skill you will need in the workplace.

Working in a second language

If you are an international student then assessments that focus on communication can be more challenging. If you are unsure, discuss the expectations of the task with your tutor. Assessment criteria may use more ambiguous terms as often there is an element of creativity identified in these forms of assessment. Make sure you understand exactly what is being assessed and don't be afraid to ask! Specific tips for writing and speaking skills are given in Parts 2 and 3.

Working with dyslexia

If you have dyslexia then you should register with the student support officer at your university. Universities provide a number of learning aids to help you in your studies. *Studying with Dyslexia* in this series will also be a valuable resource. This book will help you (and your group members) understand the characteristics of dyslexia and identify best working practices to get the most out of your studies. Students with dyslexia have poorer short-term memory, and easily miss appointments (perhaps a group member can remind you on the day, or meet with you before group meetings so you do not miss them). However, you may have an excellent long-term memory (this is not affected by dyslexia). You will also need more time to take notes and read sources, but you may be much more efficient at specific tasks such as understanding and extracting information from audio sources, for example. Identify your strengths and work to them.

What next?

If you have worked through the workshops so far, you should feel well prepared to get started on producing your poster or presentation. If you still have some thinking and planning to do, go back through Part 1 and revisit those sections you feel less confident about. Remember the 6 Ps! Once you are happy you know what your tutor wants, which skills and knowledge you are being asked to demonstrate, and the assessment criteria your tutor will use to assess these, then you are ready to move on to the 'doing' stage.

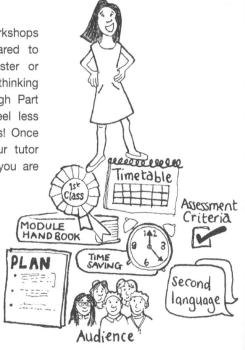

4

Introduction to posters

Part 2 shows you how to apply the core processes covered in Part 1 (thinking and planning) to creating a brilliant poster (the 'doing').

Take a look around you. From high street adverts to the Student Union, posters are a punchy and powerful way of communicating key ideas quickly and effectively. This form of undergraduate coursework develops

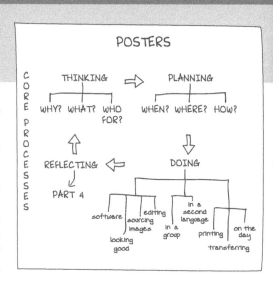

POSTERS

C O R E   P R O C E S S E S

THINKING ⟹ PLANNING

WHY? WHAT? WHO FOR?   WHEN? WHERE? HOW?

REFLECTING ⟸ DOING

PART 4

software   editing   sourcing images   in a group   in a second language   printing   on the day

looking good   transferring

your visual and written communication skills. Later, these skills will be useful in areas as diverse as improving the look of your professional portfolio and your online social networking sites.

Why have I been asked to create a poster?

Distil the essence of your argument

Wording concisely

Visual presentation skills

Teamwork

Communicate a single message clearly

What do people use posters for?

Show staff and student research in the department

Academic conferences

Recruit participants for studies

Political campaigns

Advertise products, clubs, events, gigs, shows …

Public health warnings

Posters are good for your health

> **Posters build your confidence.** You will develop your visual presentation skills and have an opportunity to practise asking and answering questions one-to-one with your tutor.

> **Posters organise your thoughts.** It takes great skill and clarity of thought to present complex ideas in a few words and pictures.

> **Posters get you friends.** You will often work in a group on your poster, and there may be a peer assessment exercise, where students read and quiz each other about their posters.

This chapter is designed to get you **thinking** about the 'why' and 'what' of creating a poster for your target audience ('who').

Posters can have extreme impact, changing people's thoughts and behaviours in significant ways. Election campaigns, health campaigns and major social, sporting and entertainment events will all be supported by posters. Don't underestimate their value.

Why are you making a poster?

→ WHY?

Student assessment

● To develop your visual presentation skills; be assessed on your learning and demonstrate you meet the learning outcomes; test ideas (especially at the early stages of their development); practise discussing ideas with tutors and other students; build confidence in answering questions.

Extracurricular activities

● To inform peers about your university club; advertise social or fund-raising events you are organising; persuade people to vote for you in the Student Union election.

Conference

● To tell experts about your research and future plans; build your national and international professional network; get feedback from experts on your thesis; get answers to questions you are stuck on. Later, this may go on the departmental wall for colleagues to read.

Job interview

● Job offer or placement.

In your first year of study you may well be given a title for the poster and very specific instructions. Your job is to provide the text and images to demonstrate your ability to locate and identify relevant information, and present a structured argument that reflects the topic of the title.

As you move towards your final years of study you may be expected to identify appropriate topics for a poster and work more independently. You may also find you need to make posters outside university for other purposes. Regardless of your year of study, Workshop 1 (p. 4) will help you identify why you are doing your poster.

What is your poster about?

Workshops 2–4 (pp. 8, 10 and 16) took you through the process of identifying what your poster is about and how to read the assignment guidelines and assessment criteria, paying particular attention to the 'process words'. You need a clear message, supported by focused, consistent argument with logical progression throughout.

The staff marking your poster use this form of communication for very practical purposes across a range of disciplines:

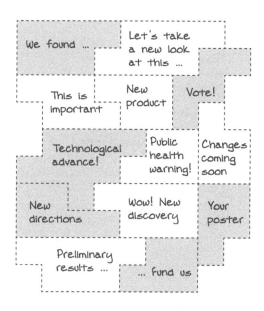

(Miracle 2003; Trimble 2010; Christenbery and Latham 2013)

Be clear what your message is – let nothing detract from it!

→ WHAT?

Student assessment

- I have developed good visual communication skills and can use software to create a good poster. I can follow guidelines and have worked hard to meet all of the assessment criteria. I have good subject knowledge. I am able to extract and process information in the way requested and can summarise key points from a range of sources.

Extracurricular activities

- This is what we do. What we do is fun/productive/enhancing/ important to you and your values. When and how to join us/vote for us.

Conference poster

- This is what I do and this is my contribution to the research field.

Employment portfolio

- This is the skill set I have to offer your company. I have good visual display skills, produce good products and have excellent organisational abilities.

Who is your audience?

In Workshop 5 (p. 18) you identified the different audiences for your poster: the person marking your work and a second 'imagined audience'. Make sure you are clear about the different audiences and what each is looking for.

For some audiences, you will need to grab their attention and draw them in. Here you must focus as much on visual attractiveness, including a clear snappy title, as the content. Other audiences will have a vested interest in reading your poster. In this case you must focus on getting the in-depth content right and provide a more fully informative title.

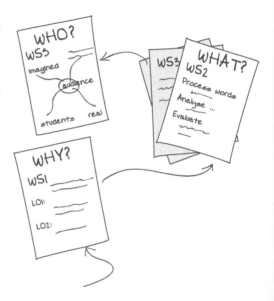

Planning how to do your poster

In Workshops 1–5 you did all the thinking and research needed to get the content of your coursework right. You identified why you are doing it (to demonstrate your learning outcomes), what you want to write (your message) and who you are writing it for (your audience). You have guidelines to follow and criteria to meet. Now you need to take this wealth of information and reduce it down to fit the limited space available in a poster. This requires careful planning!

Poster outline

Identify the logical sections of your argument. These will vary according to your subject and level of study. It is likely these will be given in the guidance notes. If you are not given section headings, think of the poster as an illustrated version of the abstract and structure it accordingly.

Poster outline:
Identify the logical
sections.

Brief background
including theoretical
framework

Brief methods

Main findings

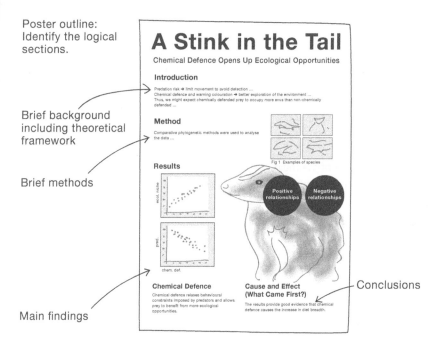

A Stink in the Tail

Chemical Defence Opens Up Ecological Opportunities

Introduction

Predation risk → limit movement to avoid detection ...
Chemical defence and warning colouration → better exploration of the environment ...
Thus, we might expect chemically defended prey to occupy more envs than non-chemically defended ...

Method

Comparative phylogenetic methods were used to analyse the data ...

Fig 1 Examples of species

Results

Positive relationships

Negative relationships

Chemical Defence

Chemical defence relaxes behavioural constraints imposed by predators and allows prey to benefit from more ecological opportunities.

Cause and Effect (What Came First?)

The results provide good evidence that chemical defence causes the increase in diet breadth.

Conclusions

Workshop 6: Bite-size chunks

Breaking the content down into smaller sections will make the job more manageable.

→ Take a sheet of paper and write the message or title in the centre.

→ Write the names of the main poster sections around the outside (include marks allocated or maximum word counts if known).

→ Bullet-point keywords and main arguments for each section.

→ Bullets can be expanded to short paragraphs.

① INTRODUCTION
- Picture - topic.
- Set the scene. ← review what we know/topic/problem
- Background info.
- Citations. ← evidence-based
- Finish with aims.

② METHODS ← what you did (keep it short!)
- Picture apparatus.
- Main method. ← use visuals to convey meaning (reduces words!)
- Sample size.
- Statistics used.

③ RESULTS ← what you found
- Graph.
- Main result.
- Statistical output.

④ DISCUSSION ← what it means
- Summarise funding.
- What does it mean?
- What next? ← what next...

STOP! Before you go any further, take out and read your notes from Workshops 1–5. Are you still on track, or have you deviated from your original plan? Be thorough, and be honest with yourself. Add and remove bullets to make sure the focus of the poster is right for this assignment. Remove non-essential information and add any keywords you missed out.

Planning when to do your poster

Deadlines

In Part 1, we suggested it is a good idea to plan your university year in terms of coursework deadlines. Take your university year planner, or diary, and find the section between now and your poster deadline. With thinking, researching and planning time included (plus all the other commitments you have), your poster will take longer to produce than you probably think. Many academics consider posters take longer to prepare than presentations – up to 8 weeks (Berg 2005; Christenbery and Latham 2013).

Workshop 7: Countdown

→ Take your year planner and/or diary and select the weeks between today and your poster deadline.

→ Make sure you have blocked out all holidays, work shifts, family days, and days when you are in lectures, working to other coursework deadlines or otherwise engaged. Be realistic!

→ The blank spaces are now your available time to work on the poster. There may not be many, so you need to plan well. See pages 20 and 83 for examples.

Plan backwards from the deadline:

Hand-in: If you have to hand in a hard copy, where must this be done, when is the location open, when can you get there?

Printing: Check the university print queue for large printers. What is the wait time?

Tutor feedback: If this is available, there will be a deadline.

Feedback from family and friends: Allow 3–4 days. People are busy.

Editing: This takes longer than you think. Expect to spend at least a day fiddling with font sizes, aligning text boxes, sizing figures, altering colour schemes.

'**Doing**': Getting the visual look and layout right is key to making a good first impression. We cover this in Chapter 7 – as you will see, there is a lot to it, as there also is to …

> **'Thinking'** and **'planning'**: Getting the message and content right is essential for working effectively and impressing your tutor. The more time you dedicate to the thinking (researching!) and planning in the first instance, the less time you waste rethinking and changing plans later on.

Spend your time wisely

Visual appearance and the title will create the first impression, but *the content will determine the lasting opinion* (Berg 2005; Rowe and Ilic 2009) and the *final mark*.

Points mean prizes! If you have been given a set of marks for each section of the poster then you should divide your effort between the different sections accordingly. The section marks will tell you where you need to focus your time and effort. Do not spend 80% of your time making your poster look nice when only 20% of the marks are for the visual component.

Planning where to work on your poster

Where you work best is an individual matter. If you need to access computers that run specialist graphics software or statistical packages, there may be limited access – so plan ahead. If you are working in a group, find a location where you can talk without disturbing others.

Consider finding a computer connected to a projector so that you can display a large image of the poster on a screen. This will help show up formatting errors that do not show on a smaller computer screen. There may also be limitations on when and where you can print your poster, especially if it is in colour and large sized. Are there laminating facilities available? Where can you buy poster tubes (if needed)?

And, of course, if you are working in a group, plan who is going to work on each section!

Once you have a good poster plan, you are ready to start creating the poster itself. Chapter 7 shows you how!

7 Doing

Which software?

Most courses recommend widely available packages such as Microsoft PowerPoint, or the Adobe design packages. Other packages are also available (e.g. LaTeX for Linux users). Software will be freely available on university computers.

For 3D graphics you will need specialist software such as the Autodesk 3ds Max 3D modelling and rendering package, or SolidWorks 3D CAD for 3D models and technical drawings. Adobe Photoshop can be used to create rendered 2D sketches and refine other graphical work. Again, if you need to use these, access will be provided by your university.

Electronic posters (e-posters) are growing in popularity in practice-driven subject areas such as medicine and the creative industries, where video conveys more useful information than 2D text and graphics. E-posters may be streamed from the internet and can be viewed on smartphones and tablet computers anytime and anywhere, with or without audio (Shin 2013). They vary from a single slide containing different elements (scrolling text, video, animated charts or 3D rotating models) presented on touch-screen monitor to a limited number of slides which viewers may scroll through.

Looking good!

First impressions count. Your audience (marker) will get frustrated if your poster looks cluttered, contains clashing colours, or is hard to read (it will take longer to mark and they will likely ask you more questions!). You want the person reading (marking!) your poster to think:

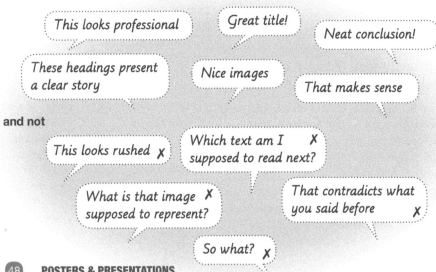

Get inspired

The best way to learn what looks good is to look at lots of posters and see what you like. For inspiration, check out staff posters in your department, at conferences, or online resources such as learned societies. www.ePosters.net is an open-access online journal of scientific posters. The site shows prize-winning posters from a range of conferences, as well as having a search facility. *Science* magazine prints winners from the annual International Science & Engineering Visualization Challenge (e.g. *Science* 2013).

Format

- Create a template and work in the correct format from the start.
- Size and orient the poster according to the instructions.
- Know your word limit and stick to it.
- Identify essential information to include (student names, word count, references, university logo?). If the university has an official poster template (available from your university website) you could consider using this. Check with your tutor first.

Layout and composition

- Use 'the rule of thirds': divide your poster into three columns and rows. Place the most important sections (main message, results, graphs, outputs) near the central four points.
- Remember that balance is more important than symmetry.
- Bear in mind that most cultures read from left to right, top to bottom, so this is the scan path the eyes will automatically want to travel.
- Have vertical columns of text to aid reading.
- Use empty space ('negative space') to frame sections and make the poster look organised and well designed.

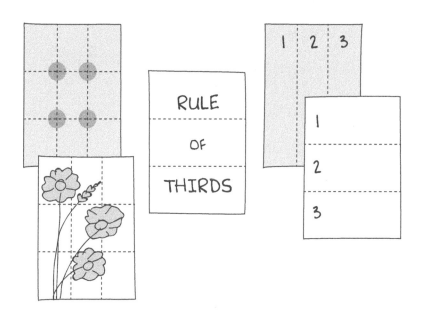

- Save space with bullet points and short sentences. Use no more than 10 lines of text in a paragraph.
- Know when to use images instead of words.

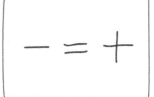

Font

Size matters!

- Your title must be readable from 5–10 m away (font size 90–144 point).
- Text must be readable from 1–2 m away (font size 16–30 point).
- Use a clear sans serif font with large inner space (i.e. the space inside the loops of letters such as 'o','d' and 'p'). Calibri, Arial and Verdana are good examples.
- Be harmonious – use one font throughout.

Look at the following examples of real posters for ideas on how to apply these rules.

Title (90–144)

Heading (30–90)

Subheading (30–60)

Text text text text
text text text text (16–30)
text text text text

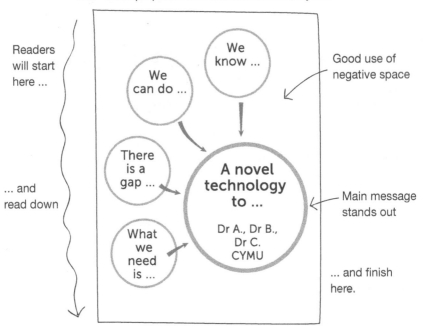

This 'concept' poster has a non-traditional layout

Readers will start here ...

... and read down

We can do ...

We know ...

There is a gap ...

A novel technology to ...

Dr A., Dr B., Dr C. CYMU

What we need is ...

Good use of negative space

Main message stands out

... and finish here.

POWERFUL COMPACT STYLISH

The AirPro 2000 hair dryer features the best in modern design, performance and style. With a high power 2000w motor, two variable heat settings and cool shot the AirPro 2000 is fast drying and innovative with a lightweight construction meaning it is a dryer you can rely on.

The integrated concentrator nozzle provides precise and professional styling no matter hair length or style making it possible to concentrate on all areas of the hair for professional results.

AIRPRO 2000

ABS barrel casing injection moulded in two parts with aluminium coated finish.

Transparent ABS nozzle attachment for concentrated air flow on all areas of the hair.

ABS air intake inlet, injection moulded with aluminium coated finish, allowing air to continuously flow through the dryer.

Textured rubber handle for comfortable grip, situated around the centre of the barrel.

ABS power control buttons injection moulded with aluminium coated finish.

AIRPRO 2000

AVAILABLE IN AN ARRAY OF VIBRANT COLOURS TO ACCOMMODATE USER PREFERENCES.

AIRPRO 2000

Safeguarding Children Workshop

Multi-professional Learning and Networking – Creating a Community of Practice

Introduction

"Safeguarding children … is everyone's responsibility."[1] (p7)

Everyone who comes into contact with children…has a role to play.[1] (p7)

- Multi-agency co-operation needs to improve[3,4].

Multi-professional learning in higher education – developing future professionals

Learning together and from one another supports the development of learning communities.

- Wenger (2000)[5] validates the value of communities of practice as "basic building blocks of a social learning system"[5] (p229).
- Tang and Biggs[6] discussion on constructive alignment supports the value of learning communities[6]. This workshop, aimed at students of nursing, midwifery, paramedics, teaching, mental health, social work and policing studies, enhances employability[8] and facilitates joint learning and working – in the best interest of service users.
- Improving employability[8] and reflecting the professional reality of joint learning and working – in the best interest of service users –Students are motivated by the need to know and by trying to understand the meaning of the bigger picture, both essential for deep learning[6].

Context

"Children are best protected when professionals are clear about what is required of them individually, and how they need to work together."[1] (pg 7)

Benefits of establishing a community of practice

- Students develop through expert knowledge and peer learning.
- Opening up inclusive ways to develop students' and their professionalism conforming to The Quality Assurance Agency's[9] Chapter B indicators 1, 3 and 6 and the Higher Education Academy's UK Professional Standards Framework[10] dimensions K1, 2 and 3.
- Reinforcing multi-professional collaboration required by the Children Act 2004[11].
- Professional standards, e.g. Nursing and Midwifery Council[12] and Teachers' Standards[13] and associated courses focus on service user protection. Multi-professional safeguarding teaching is currently not part of the curriculum.
- Networking and collaboration prepare for employment[3,8].

Working Together to Safeguard Children
Multi-professional practice workshop

No single profession can effectively safeguard children.

You are invited to develop your multi-professional knowledge and skills, to update your understanding of safeguarding children, to network and to explore opportunities for collaboration.

Wednesday, 16th October 2013, 9am–12:30pm

Room 5.04 Tithebarn Street

Tea/coffee will be provided, please e-mail m.bird@ljmu.ac.uk if you wish to attend.
Faculty of Health and Applied Social Sciences: Social Work; Avril Robarts Centre

Aim and Objectives of the Workshop

Aim – to increase students' awareness of safeguarding children and the role of multi-agency co-operation.

Increasing knowledge and understanding of safeguarding	Exploring multi-agency duties, roles and responsibilities	Building multi-professional networks

Establish a community of practice focused on safeguarding

Implementation

Pilot phase – optional offer to all final year undergraduate and postgraduate students. 60 places are available in line with average attendance at multi-professional practice seminars.

Planning and organization –

- Establish a baseline of safeguarding teaching across professional programmes to pitch the workshop at the right level
- Plan with academic staff from target professional programmes, confirm facilitators, keynote speaker and final agenda
- Disseminate invitation to students

On the day –

- Keynote speech by safeguarding expert
- Three workshops: "Professional value base"; "Roles and responsibilities" and "Information sharing" co-facilitated by representatives from different programmes' safeguarding teams

Evaluation –

- Observation by co-facilitators
- Immediate response survey completed at the end of the event

Moving Forward

Meeting students' long-term learning needs is the decisive element in evaluating the effectiveness of this curriculum development[7]

Research cafe

- A research cafe will provide the opportunity to elaborate on the initial survey responses to elicit richer qualitative data. The "merit, worth and significance"[14] (p631) of the pilot workshop can be verified by reflecting on its design and its outcomes[7]. Co-constructing teaching and learning will enhance and improve future workshops of this community of practice.

✔ Learning from students' views the concept of this workshop – learning together and from one another.

✔ Students' feedback supports the facilitators' transformative reflective practice[6] and professional development[7].

➡ **Roll out workshop**

Reflective Learning at Masters Level
The use of Reflective Diaries to assess personal development modules
Assessment of personal development in vocational Masters courses: Are essays and reports suitable vehicles?

Reflection is an accepted part of learning but one that is infrequently assessed directly. Kolb (1984) places it with equal emphasis on planning, conceptualisation and acting. Schon (1987) argued that the application of theory within professional practice is driven by reflection – making tacit knowledge explicit to allow it to be considered and improved. Moon (2005), writing for the HEA believes that reflection in assessment requires careful thought and planning, especially around assessment criteria. But that, carefully managed, can, "deepen their reflection to levels from which greater value will develop." (p.3). Reflection in assessment supports HEA values, especially A, B & E.

> We do not learn from experience … we learn from reflecting on experience (Dewey, 1953:78)

Statement of the problem. The MSc in Entrepreneurship is a new programme to be run from September 2013, aimed at students intending to start their own business. There has been extended debate on the role of universities in teaching entrepreneurship. Kirby (2004:510) stated that, " the traditional education system stultifies rather than develops the requisite attributes and skills to produce entrepreneurs", so to combat this, the module, Psychology of Entrepreneurship has been developed. Students are required to:
- Demonstrate insight into own strengths and development areas relating to building and running a business.
- Critically evaluate & apply a range of self-presentation techniques effectively. These learning outcomes require an proactive and innovative method of assessing the learning outcomes (Kickul and Fayolle, 2007:1).

The intervention
Knowles et al. (2012:16) explored the use of reflective diaries by practitioners and concluded that, "critical reflection carries true potential to bring about change, be it change at a personal level or change across professions".
Therefore a reflective diary, weighted at 40% of the mark, will be used to assess reflection on this new module. It will be introduced with clear instructions around reflection using the Gibbs (1988) reflection framework and the professional impact assessment recommended by Gahye and Lilleyman (2006). An exercise in agreeing assessment criteria will be integral to improve student understanding of the process.
The reflective diary will chart the students' journey towards increased self-awareness through the coaching and self-awareness activities and practical applications embedded in the programme. This is in line with HEA values , especially E and SEDA values, especially 1, 2, 5 and 6.

How will we know if it works?
The ultimate measure of success will be more graduates starting, growing and maturing their businesses, an outcome taking a number of years to assess.

At an individual level, the intervention will be a success if it **demonstrates achievement of the learning outcomes**. Measures of this include awareness of personal strengths and areas for improvement, the production of a development action plan rooted in the reflective process and a demonstration of distance travelled during the process of writing the reflective diary.

To provide context for the success and to drive improvements at a programme level, students will be interviewed to assess their perceptions of writing reflectively and its effects on their learning.

The findings of these interviews will combined with the individual outcomes and used to assess the effectiveness of reflective diaries in learning on this module. They will also help to shape and refine the process and assessment in future years as recommended by Tang (2002).

Why assess using a reflective diary rather than an essay?

	Assessment by Essay	Assessment by Diary
Positives	• Encourages organisation of knowledge, integration of theory and expression of opinions • Encourages thinking about what and how • Helpful for assessing complex learning outcomes – application, synthesis and evaluation of concepts • Promotes active learning	• Promotes deep and critical thinking • Encourages thinking on what, how and why • Enables students to learn from experience, feeding forward into continuous personal and professional development • Promotes active learning
Negatives/Problems	• Learning about what has happened and drawing conclusions rather than planning how the future might be different. • Easy to mark	• Personal • Unfamiliar to students, requires specific guidance on a new way of thinking • Difficult to mark

Colour

Use colour to highlight important content and draw attention to your poster. Use a few colours, and use them well.

- Use high-contrast colours (dark/light) for the text and background.
- People are used to reading dark text on a light background.
- Plain backgrounds are less distracting than textured backgrounds.
- Use colour to unite poster components (e.g. all text or all headings in the same colour).
- Use bright colours wisely; they grab attention, but can also distract readers.
- Use a colour wheel for inspiration on colour combining, e.g. https://kuler.adobe.com/#explore/newest/?time=all
- Using continuous and hatched lines on graphs may help distinguish lines more effectively than different colours.

Colour blindness

Avoid combining red with green. Approximately 8% of the world's population has a form of colour vision deficiency (CVD) and red–green colour blindness is the most common form: www.colourblindawareness.org. You can see what your poster would look like to someone with CVD using an onscreen filter such as http://colororacle.org/.

Sourcing images

▸ Use a few good quality images.
▸ Only use copyright-free images. These include figures or photos you have created yourself or images from one of the copyright-free sources listed below.
▸ Never use images from the internet or any other source that you do not have permission to use.
▸ To ensure an image is good quality, always save it before inserting it into a document.
▸ Never download images from a website by right-clicking (they will be poor quality).
▸ Always cite the source of images on your poster. Check with your tutor on the format for image citations.

Useful sources of copyright-free images

▸ MorgueFile: http://www.morguefile.com/
▸ Wikimedia Commons: Archive of free multimedia content submitted by Wikipedia users. http://commons.wikimedia.org/wiki/Main_Page
▸ JISC MediaHub collection: http://jiscmediahub.ac.uk/
▸ Google Images using the 'usage rights' filter. http://images.google.com/advanced_image_search

- FreeFoto.com: A collection of free photographs for private non-commercial use. http://www.freefoto.com/index.jsp
- Image*After: large, free photo collection, with images free for any use. http://www.imageafter.com/
- Creative Commons: Searches material that is licensed under the Creative Commons. http://search.creativecommons.org/

Editing

Once completed, leave your poster for a few days and come back to it with a fresh eye. Errors will jump off the page at you. Remember that you will lose marks for misaligned sections, misspellings and poor quality images.

- Scan around the poster on screen and correct any mistakes.
- Check the resolution of pictures by displaying them at 100% size on the screen. Anything less than 300 dpi may look unfocused once scaled up and printed.
- Print a copy (in black and white and A4 or A3 size for editing purposes).
- Printing larger formats – and printing in colour – costs more, and uses more resources, so print wisely.
- Turn the printout upside down to check column alignments and balance of layout. This will help you focus on the layout rather than the text.

Handouts

You may be asked to provide A4 handouts of your poster. Printing in black and white is cheaper and more environmentally friendly, but your colourful poster may look cluttered in shades of grey, so try the following.

- Create a separate version (A4 size) of your poster for the handout.
- Set the format to black text on a white background.
- Reduce the amount of text and increase the font size. Use bullet points.
- Print enough copies for your tutors and fellow students.

Any questions?

You will probably be asked questions about your poster: either by your tutor as part of the assessment, or by fellow students as part of a reflective learning exercise.

Your tutor will ask questions to test your knowledge. Make sure you understand the poster. Be clear about the rationale and main message. Avoid using terms you do not understand (or look them up!). If you present statistical analyses, make sure you understand why you chose those tests, and what the output means.

Practise answering questions from family, friends and your group. Write their questions down and practise answering them.

Workshop 8: Doing

Create a template in PowerPoint (or your specialist software)

	Done?
	☑
→ Set your poster size (e.g. A0, A1, A2). You can do this under the 'Design' tab in PowerPoint.	☐
→ Set the orientation (landscape or portrait).	☐
→ Set a plain, pale background colour.	☐
→ Select a single font in a dark colour.	☐

Composition and content

→ Divide the poster space into a grid ('rule of thirds')	☐
→ Create a title banner across the top.	☐
→ Insert your title in large bold text, centred.	☐
→ Create text boxes for each section of the poster.	☐
→ Insert the main headings, images, figures, tables, text, students' names, logos and any other required information.	☐
→ Size your headings, text, figures and tables.	☐

Editing

→ Edit thoroughly to reduce text while maintaining depth of content. ☐
→ Check for grammatical and spelling mistakes. ☐
→ Adjust your colour scheme to best highlight important information. ☐
→ Check quality of images at 100% size on the screen. ☐
→ Print a copy and turn upside down to check alignment of text
   boxes and images, good use of negative space and balance of sections. ☐
→ Turn the printout upside down to check if it looks cluttered or if
   there is too much space. ☐
→ Once you are happy with the revised content and layout, leave it for
   a few days and come back to it for a final check-over before printing. ☐

Doing posters in a second language

Making posters in your second (or third) language presents an additional challenge. It is likely your tutor will grant you some leeway for grammatical and spelling errors initially, but assessment criteria will become more stringent as you progress through your studies.

It is important that your written text is precise and concise. If in doubt, make use of student support and proofreading services available at your university. Once you start creating posters to communicate with the outside world you need your text to read well.

Ask friends and other students who are native speakers to read the text and help with editing it. Visuals and examples are especially important when there is a potential language barrier of any kind.

Make sure you also practise answering questions poster viewers are likely to ask. It is particularly important when not speaking in your native language to anticipate questions in advance.

Group posters

▸ Decide at the outset who is going to work on which section.
▸ Every student should contribute to, and be able to comment on, all sections.
▸ Allocate each member of the group a word limit for their section.
▸ Make sure all contributions are in the same format (font, style, colour, size).
▸ One person should edit the text of the poster to ensure it reads as if written by a single person. Check there are no sudden changes in tense or writing style.
▸ Refer to the assignment guidelines when making group decisions. You must adhere to these and they are useful for resolving (inevitable) differences of opinion.

Workshop 9: Workshop recap

Before you print (or submit) your poster, take out your notes from WS 1–5.

→ Have you demonstrated the learning outcomes? (WS1)
→ Have you followed the assignment guidelines and answered the question (addressed the process words)? (WS2)
→ Have you done enough background reading and do your poster title and content convey your core message clearly? (WS3)
→ Does it meet all of the assessment criteria? (WS4)
→ Is it pitched correctly for your audience? (WS5)

Printing

There may be a queue for the limited number of printers that can print larger poster sizes (such as A0), so you may need to send your poster a few days (rather than hours) before the deadline.

 Transporting posters is always tricky as they are large and cumbersome. You need a poster tube large enough to fit the poster, and you need to carry this with you. If you have far to walk you will want a carrier with a strap.

On the day

Dress smartly. This is your opportunity to present yourself as a knowledgeable, confident, capable, vibrant, promising student. Be prepared to answer questions. If you are providing copies of abstracts (see *Planning Your Dissertation* and *Report Writing* in this series for tips on composing an abstract), a reference list (see *Referencing and Understanding Plagiarism*), or A4 printouts for your tutor or other students (see the section on handouts above, p. 61), make sure you have enough to go around the class.

Once you receive the mark for your poster, work through Part 4 to reflect on your feedback and improve on your performance in future assessments.

Introduction to presentations

Part 3 shows you how to apply the core processes covered in Part 1 (thinking and planning) to creating a polished presentation (the 'doing').

Whether on the television or internet, in a lecture theatre or a public space, the spoken word is a powerful tool. As a form

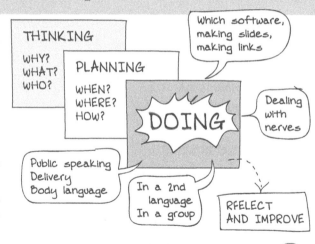

THINKING

WHY?
WHAT?
WHO?

PLANNING

WHEN?
WHERE?
HOW?

DOING

Which software, making slides, making links

Dealing with nerves

Public speaking
Delivery
Body language

In a 2nd language
In a group

RFELECT AND IMPROVE

of undergraduate coursework, presentations develop your verbal, as well as visual and written, communication skills. You will learn to engage and to connect with people and ultimately build a working relationship. Later, these skills will help impress job interviewers, and improve communication in the work setting and other public-speaking situations.

Why have I been asked to create a presentation?

What do people use presentations for?

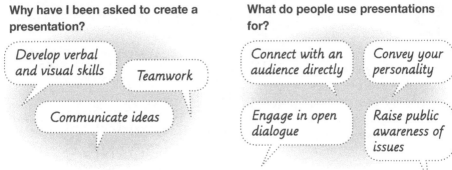

Develop verbal and visual skills

Teamwork

Communicate ideas

Connect with an audience directly

Convey your personality

Engage in open dialogue

Raise public awareness of issues

Your chance to shine

Talking in front of a group is what university lecturers and schoolteachers do every day. So, it can't be that bad, right? Talking, telling and teaching others is rewarding. Once you have given a few presentations and got over the nerves, you may even find you enjoy it!

As with posters, we want to help you think about the *why*, *what* and *who* of giving a presentation. These chapters will help you identify the key areas to be addressed and steps that need to be taken in designing and delivering a presentation.

Why are you making a presentation?

You are making a presentation to:

- develop your visual presentation and public-speaking skills
- be assessed on your learning and demonstrate you meet the learning outcomes
- present work or research that you have done (usually at the end of a project)
- test well-formulated ideas and get immediate feedback
- be asked questions that will further develop your thinking.

In order for your presentation to make the right impact, you must be very clear about its purpose. At university, most presentations you deliver will be assessed. As you move into your final year you may make a presentation at a conference, or it could form part of the interview process for a job. Workshop 1 (p. 4) will help you identify why you are doing a presentation.

Context	Type	Aims
Student assessment	Short presentation on topic set by lecturer.	Demonstrate you meet the learning outcomes, understand the subject and can communicate your ideas verbally.
Extracurricular activities	Short address to other students regarding club or society or election to office.	Persuade fellow students to join or vote for you through the persuasiveness of your argument.
Conference presentation	Short lecture based on an aspect of research to inform experts in your field.	Show that you are able to communicate your research verbally and summarise your research visually.
Job interview	Short seminar summarising main features of your study or research programme to inform and influence prospective employer.	Demonstrate your communication skills in a professional context.

What is your presentation about?

To make a really effective presentation you need to present a simple and clear message. What do you want your audience to learn? You identified your take-home message in Workshops 2–4 (pp. 8, 10 and 16). Remember the importance of addressing the 'process words' in university assignments (see p. 6). It is important that you consider how you are going to use your presentation to convey your message, make the right impression and gain that good grade you are after.

Your verbal presentation skills will be useful in a range of real-world settings, such as those shown opposite.

> The power of the spoken word is evident in the number of famous speeches that have moved, inspired and roused people throughout history. See some examples by following this link: http://list25.com/25-speeches-that-changed-the-world/.

Making the right impression means not only putting together good slides but also considering the way in which your speech supports the material on the slides and how you link from one section to the next. The visual and verbal should complement each other in conveying your message.

Who is your audience?

In Workshop 5 (p. 18) you identified different audiences for your presentation. You need to consider the tutor, the imagined audience and your fellow students. You must pitch your presentation at the appropriate level to ensure impact. This is particularly important for presentations, as you will be facing your real and student audiences as you deliver the material.

Context	Audience and knowledge	What do they want?
Student assessment	Lecturer and your classmates. All will be knowledgeable but lecturer will be assessing the knowledge.	Lecturer wants to see that you can communicate your ideas to a group verbally using appropriate images; to see your enthusiasm, interest and passion for your topic; to test your deeper knowledge through your responses to questions. Other students will want to learn what you did, what you found and what you think about it.

Context	Audience and knowledge	What do they want?
Extracurricular activities	Students interested in the club or society. Student voters in student elections.	To see what your club does, brought to life; to get a feel for the personality of members and character of the club as a whole; to be convinced that it is worth joining your club/society or that you are an electable officer.
Conference presentation	Mostly experts in your field or a related area of study.	To learn about latest developments in the field and future directions – including your research findings and 'next step'.
Job interview	Potential employer and possible future work colleagues.	To see you how you communicate verbally and with body language; how you deal with stressful situations and cope under pressure; how you articulate your personal and professional strengths in a professional context; to get a feel for your personality and whether they would like to have you 'on their team'.

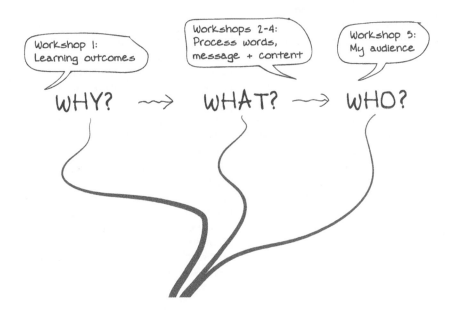

Planning how to do your presentation

Getting the content right is critical, and you worked on this in Workshops 1–5. Now you need to prepare the slides and work out what you are going to say, and how to say it effectively. An approximate timescale for working on each part of the presentation is given here:

Research time	10 hours for every 15 minutes of presentation
Visual preparation	30 minutes to 1 hour for each slide
Practice time	4 hours, to include two full run-throughs of the presentation

Presentation outline

Having thoroughly researched your topic, and with a clear idea of what you want to say, you can start the process of structuring the presentation (working out what you will say when). As with posters, work to the principle that *less is more* (p. 52). It is natural to want to demonstrate how much you know by delivering as much material as possible in the time allowed. However, an over-complicated presentation conveys that you are not clear about your main message. A straightforward presentation with a clear message will be better understood and appreciated (as long as you do your research and have depth of content!).

You should also consider the transitions between different speakers. Make sure you include this in the presentation plan. Seamless links from one speaker to the next will keep the narrative alive and maintain a dynamic and engaging show that captures and maintains the audience's attention.

When structuring the talk outline you need to be clear about the purpose and aims of the presentation.

An effective talk outline is:

> *Tell 'em … tell 'em … told 'em.*
> Tell your audience what you are going to say. Tell them. Then tell your audience what you have told them.

PowerPoint slide organisation

You may be given very specific instructions about what should go on each slide. If this is not provided, use the structure given below. A general rule is to allow about 2 minutes per slide. So, for a 15-minute talk, you should aim to use seven or eight slides plus the title and final slide – so nine or ten in total.

Introduction

The title slide allows you to develop your opening, and introduce yourself/selves and the title of the talk. The second slide (start of the introduction) is then crucial. You need to hold the audience's attention and lay a clear foundation for the presentation. A list of what to explain is given here:

▶ *How you are going to talk about it*: What evidence you are presenting – for example, results of an experiment, review of the literature.
▶ *What you expect the audience to do*: For example, refer to the handouts, ask questions throughout, leave discussion to the end.

Middle section

This is where you present your argument. Make sure that this section is:

▶ coherently structured so that the audience can engage with your delivery
▶ limited to three to four main sequential points that proceed in a logical way; each point should build from the previous point(s)
▶ aligned with your title, introduction and conclusion
▶ structured into a clear, authoritative discussion.

Conclusion

Having held your audience's attention, you need to make a positive lasting impression. In your conclusion:

▶ Return to the title and the subject area: *'This talk focused on ...'*
▶ Summarise the evidence you presented. *'A series of experiments was undertaken ...'*
▶ Deliver a definitive conclusion: *'The results show ...', 'We can conclude ...'*
▶ Thank the audience for their attention. You may also want to direct questions: *'I am happy to take questions and would be particularly grateful to receive comments on the research methodology ...'*

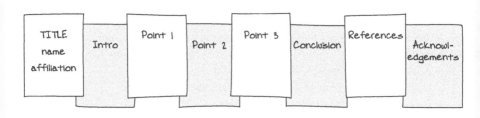

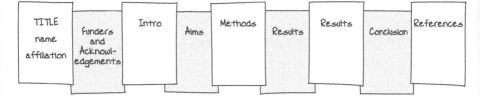

> ## Workshop 10: Bite-size chunks
>
> Breaking the content down into smaller sections will make the job more manageable.
> → Take a sheet of paper and write the message or title in the centre.
> → Write the names of the main presentation sections around the outside (include marks allocated for each section if known).
> → Bullet-point keywords and main arguments for each section.
> → Bullets can be expanded to full sentences.
> → Identify information you want to present visually as pictures on slides (main topic of slide), which information should be text (main points relating to the topic), and which should be spoken (extra detail to 'flesh out' the main points).

Planning when to do your presentation

Deadlines

The presentation day will be clearly written in your diary, but are there deadlines that fall before this? Do you need to submit the slides to be loaded onto a computer before the day of the presentation? Are there deadlines for tutor feedback? Do you need to submit an abstract?

Before you start, take your year planner or diary and draft a provisional timeline for your presentation. Work back from the deadline. Add dates where you may need to submit drafts or a summary. Here we show a Gantt chart, which is another way of planning the major milestones involved in doing coursework. Compare this with the picture on p. 20 and use whichever method works best for you.

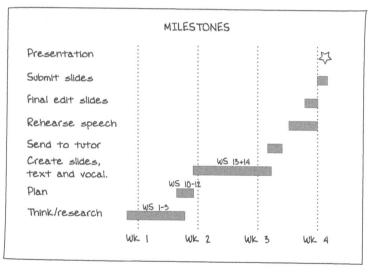

MILESTONES

Presentation

Submit slides

Final edit slides

Rehearse speech

Send to tutor

Create slides,
text and vocal.   WS 13+14

Plan   WS 10-12

Think/research   WS 1-5

Wk 1   Wk 2   Wk 3   Wk 4

Workshop 11: Countdown

→ Take your calendar, diary or Gantt chart and mark in your presentation deadline.
→ Working back from the deadline to today, mark out the major milestones:

Hand-in: If you have to send a copy of your slides in advance, how do you do this? Email your tutor? Hand in a copy on a memory stick? Find out exactly what is to be sent and where/who to.

Tutor feedback: Are you able to send your tutor a draft copy of your slides, or practise your presentation with them? If so, what is the deadline for this?

Feedback from family and friends: If you want to practise your presentation, find a time (a few days in advance of the presentation day) when you can bring your friends and family together, or schedule individual practice runs.

Editing: Always takes longer than you think. Expect to spend a day fiddling with font sizes, aligning text boxes, sizing figures and altering colour schemes.

'Doing': We cover this in Chapter 11. There is a lot to it, as there is to …

'Thinking' and **'planning'**: It is likely you will change your plans at various stages of the 'doing'. The more time you dedicate to the thinking and planning in the first instance, the less time you waste rethinking and changing plans later on.

Spend your time wisely

- Do your research and get a good story.
- Make sure your message is clear.
- Identify the key 'sections' of the presentation.
- Work out exactly how long each section of your presentation takes.
- For group work, decide who will be responsible for each section.
- Review progress regularly to ensure everything is on track.
- Practise both alone and with the group.

Points mean prizes! Marks will be allocated for the content, verbal delivery and visual appearance of your presentation. You should focus your effort on these different aspects accordingly. If you are nervous about public speaking, then practise, practise, practise! Speak in front of anyone who will listen. Rehearsing in front of an audience will identify areas that are unclear, need further explanation or can be removed altogether. You will also get better at answering unexpected questions. With practice and feedback, you will learn to refine your words and text on slides and learn to use images that prompt you to remember what to talk about next. Three full run-throughs is a good target to build your confidence.

Any questions?

Plan for how to answer questions.

- Anticipate possible questions and rehearse answering them. For ideas of what questions people ask in your area of study, make a note of questions asked at the end of departmental seminars or any conferences you attend.
- Rather than say 'I don't know', show how you would find the answer to the question given a little more time: *'That is a really good question ... It was outside the remit of this study ... I expect there to be data on this ... I can check and get back to you ...'*
- If the question is about a particular point you presented, scroll back to that slide so you can refer to the relevant information as you explain your answer.
- If you are faced by what feels like aggressive or critical questioning, do not get defensive. Take a deep breath, thank the person for their question and calmly make your response.
- You may include additional slides at the end of your talk for anticipated questions about details you did not have time to include in the talk itself. This looks professional – it shows you are thorough, considered and know your topic well – and indicates to the audience you know a lot more than you had time to cover in the short time available.

It may be possible to direct questions to the audience at the end of your presentation. For example, you could ask *'Does anyone have any questions about the methodology?'* or *'We are happy to take any questions but are particularly interested in your feedback on ...'*

Time

Practise sticking to time. Be very clear about the amount of time you have. If a 20-minute time slot includes a 5-minute Q&A session at the end, you have 15 minutes for your talk. If it is a group presentation, each student should talk for the same amount of time, so divide the sections equally among you. A good tip is to have a time keeper who can signal when you have 1 minute left. By helping each other to stick to time, the last students to talk will not be in danger of having a shortened time slot for their section. Practising lots will help you keep to time and prevent you losing time umm-ing and ahh-ing, forgetting your words, rifling through your notes, or waffling until you find the point you knew you needed to make.

Planning where to work on your presentation

If you are meeting in a group, meet where you can run the slides on a computer (or on a projector screen), so everyone can see, and where you can talk noisily without disturbing others. Even when working on your own, it may be best to consider working away from other people so that you can practise speaking the words as you write your text or work on your slides. If you can, it is a good idea to practise speaking in the location where you will be assessed. Get a feeling for the space and capacity of the room. Visualise yourself giving the presentation to nodding, smiling faces, to increase your confidence.

Workshop 12: Planning a presentation

Fill in details of your presentation in the table below.

Title:		Date:
Deadlines	Abstract or summary deadline	
	Date for presentation	
Solo or group?		**Number**
	Number of people making presentation	
		Minutes
Time	How long for talking? Per person, if group	
	How long for questioning?	
		Tick if needed
Equipment	Laptop	
	Access to the internet	
	Remote slide advancer or laser pointer	

		Give details
Location	Building	
	Floor	
	Room number	
	Room type, e.g. lecture theatre, classroom	
		Give details
Audience	Number of attendees	
	Expertise of attendees	

With the whole process planned, and everyone clear on their individual roles and the group mission, it is time to start putting your well-researched material into the format of a presentation.

Identify the resources you will need to create your presentation.

Which software?

There are two primary choices for visual aids: PowerPoint or Prezi. PowerPoint is the more traditional presentation program developed by Microsoft in 1990. It is likely to be available on your university computers. Prezi is a more recent (2009), cloud-based presentation software that enables a story-telling presentation approach (http://prezi. com/). Both packages will enable you to display text and figures and embed other forms of media. See the comparison table on the next page.

If there is a spatial context to your presentation, for example geographical locations or progression of events over time, Prezi may be particularly effective. However, bear in mind that, whatever you use, the program is only as good as the presenter and there is no substitute for hard work.

	PowerPoint	**Prezi**
Access and storage	Saved on computer or memory stick. Can also be emailed. **Be aware:** Possibility of compatibility problems due to different versions of PowerPoint.	Web-based, so requires access to the internet, but can be saved offline. **Be aware:** Presentation vulnerable to network/wifi problems.
Content delivery	Linear set of slides.	Dynamic, with ability to zoom in and out of images and text on a single slide.
Customisation	High level choice, e.g. font, colour, template.	More limited choice from fixed templates.
Visual effects	Templates incorporate rectangular text boxes on rectangular slides.	More up-to-date range of design components, including circular and other shaped components.
Classic student mistakes to beware of	Do not use 'animations' in academic presentations unless they are necessary and add a professional touch to your presentation.	Avoid 'zoom fatigue'. The most effective Prezi presentations have a minimal amount of zooming around the page. Once you have zoomed into an area, spend time talking about it. Avoid zooming down too many levels – your audience will lose track of where you are in 'the bigger picture'.

Looks count!

For inspiration, think about lectures, departmental research seminars or public talks you have really enjoyed. What did the presenter do to keep your attention? What slides looked good? You probably find that dynamic speakers who talk enthusiastically about their topic without needing to refer to notes, showing slides with perhaps nothing more than a good picture on, are the ones who stand out in your mind. Try to incorporate elements of presentation style that you like into your own presentations. You can view Prezi presentations online – take a look at some of the most popular and see what you like and don't like.

Keep it simple. As with posters, 'less is more'. Limit the text. Use short sentences or bulleted 'prompt' words.

Font: Select a readable font. Use a sans serif font (without tails) for screen legibility. Use one font throughout your presentation. Use font size to create hierarchy. A larger font will indicate to the viewer where to look first.

Font size: Headings should be at least 28 point, main text at least 20 point.

Line spacing: Ensure at least 1.5 spacing between lines.

Alignment: Left aligned is easiest to read.

Case: AVOID UPPERCASE as this can look like SHOUTING and is more difficult to read.

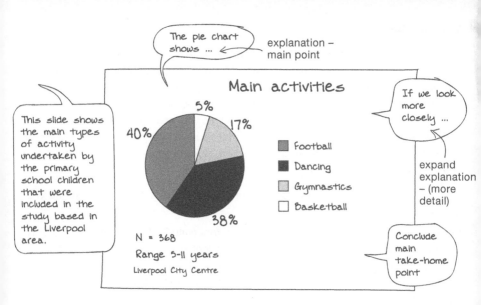

Colour: Keep it simple. Select a colour palette with contrast. For emphasis underline or embolden words rather than present them in a different colour from the rest of the text. Make sure your colour choices are not distracting.

Headers: Avoid fancy headers but include logos of any companies or institutions that have provided you with support (e.g. financial), use of specialist equipment or access to resources.

Visuals

'A picture is worth a thousand words …'

Visuals add interest. Used effectively, they can convey much meaning without you having to say anything, saving you time, engaging your audience and making your take-home message more memorable.

- Use a single, good clear image per slide and on your title slide.
- Use graphs, maps, tables or flowcharts in the main body to illustrate key points.
- Make sure all images are simple and large.
- When presenting data (e.g. graphs, tables), keep it simple so that the main point is clear; you can include full data diagrams in a handout if needed (see p. 61).
- Make sure labels are large enough to be read from the back of the room. Again, clarity is more important than detail. An axis label like 'Length (cm)' in large bold letters is enough. You can then point and talk the audience through the graph as you explain it more fully during the presentation itself.

Slides

Slide template

Keep it simple.

Avoid patterned backgrounds: these make slides look cluttered and distract attention from the important content.

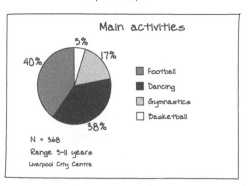

If you want to use a pre-formatted template, go for a simple theme that reflects the content and intended outcomes of your presentation.

Otherwise you should select a background colour that ensures maximum contrast with your text. Dark text on a pale background is most effective.

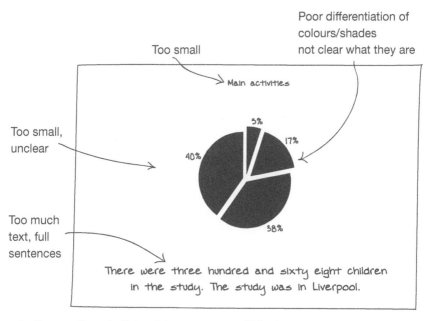

Poor differentiation of colours/shades not clear what they are

Too small

Main activities

Too small, unclear

40%

5%

17%

38%

Too much text, full sentences

There were three hundred and sixty eight children in the study. The study was in Liverpool.

Audience will read off the slide = less engaged with you

Take-home message not clear

If you are representing your institution at an external conference, you may be required to use the standard university template that forms part of your university's visual identity.

Slide transitions

'Less is more' applies to slide transitions. By transition we mean moving between points on a single slide, as well as moving from one slide to the next (or 'zooming' in Prezi).

A criticism made of PowerPoint is 'death by a thousand bullets'. Bullet points whizzing in and out with sound effects are dated and look unprofessional. Fixed slide content is easier to manage: you can point at the slide and maintain eye contact with the audience without having to look down at the clicker or mouse. Fewer animations reduce the risk of compatibility issues between your talk and the version of PowerPoint you are presenting in. Also, if you return to slides for questions at the end of the presentation you can display the entire content for each point.

When moving between slides, talk the audience through the transition by concluding the current slide and linking it to the next.

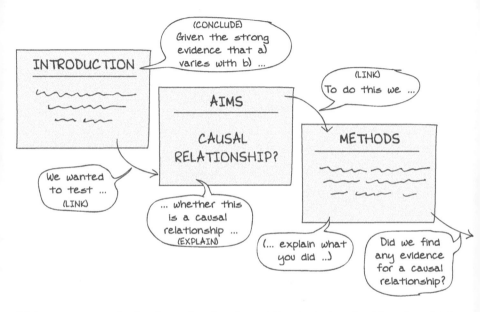

Make sure you understand – and make clear at the start of each slide – the slide's purpose. For example: *'This graph shows ...' 'This map explains the location of ...' 'This satellite image shows the scale of ...' 'Here is a picture of ...'*

In this Prezi example, the timeline is linear. The audience can clearly see where you start and finish.

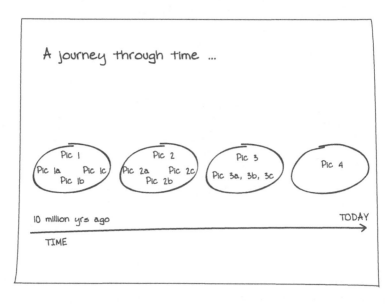

This Prezi speaks for itself …

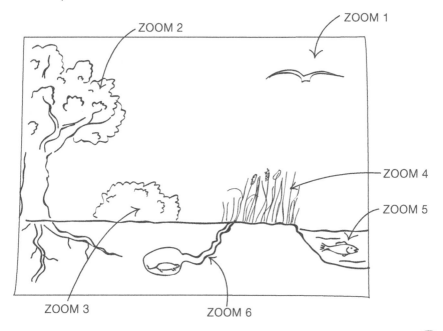

Workshop 13: Slide checklist

		☑
Font	Sans serif	☐
	Headings at least 28 point	☐
	Body at least 20 point	☐
Line spacing	At least 1.5	☐
Alignment	Left	☐
Slide template	University template required	☐
Slide transitions	Simple single slide	☐

Accessible presentations

Visual components – graphs, table, images, text – are obviously an important part of an oral presentation. Ensure that slides can be seen and understood by everyone in the room. Keep the design simple to aid inclusivity. Specific strategies for developing an inclusive presentation are given on the next page.

1 Underline or embolden important words. Do not write them in a different colour – this looks cluttered.
2 Keep high contrast between text and background. Use a dark text on a pale background.
3 Deliver the content orally. Avoid asking the audience to read quotes from the screen without you paraphrasing them and explaining the purpose of visuals and what they are showing. This will enable anyone with a visual impairment to understand your presentation.
4 Allow time for the content on each slide to be read and understood. This will be of benefit to anyone with a hearing impairment.
5 Provide handouts people can refer to.

It is important to note that an accessible presentation will be of help to everyone in your audience. Some people may have a restricted view of the slides and the acoustics may impact on the audibility of your presentation.

Delivery

Practise, practise, practise!

Where and how to stand

▶ Face the audience and not the screen.
▶ Do not obscure the slides.
▶ Adopt a stable, confident position.
▶ Keep your body language positive, open and relaxed.
▶ Do not cross your arms.
▶ Keep your head up.
▶ Use your hands deliberately to emphasise a point.

Tone

'Tone' refers to how the audience perceives the presentation. Whatever the size or composition of the audience, consider a presentation as a formal event.

▶ Introduce yourself, even if you think you know everyone in the room.
▶ Convey your professional identity and your professional 'community', for example the programme you are on, your research group, your department or your institution.
▶ Treat the presentation and the audience with respect.
▶ Dress neatly and present yourself professionally.
▶ Convey your enthusiasm for your programme or research.

Immediacy

'Immediacy' is the perceived distance between the presenter and the audience. Try not to stand behind a barrier, such as a computer or lectern. By standing away from or in front of any fixed barriers the perceived distance between you and the audience will decrease. This will help you to connect more easily with the group and make them more predisposed to your delivery.

Other non-verbal behaviours that increase immediacy are smiling, eye contact, open gesturing and relaxed body language.

Body language – top tips

Stand up straight with your arms and chest open: This will help you breathe more easily and feel more relaxed. Avoid shifting from foot to foot or leaning against something.

Smile: Be natural and sincere. This will make the audience feel comfortable and convey that you are pleased to see everyone.

Speak clearly at an audible volume: Get a friend to sit at the back and signal if you can be heard. Speaking more slowly is better than too fast. Leave pauses to allow people to process information, especially if you are referring to complex ideas or images.

Make eye contact with as many people as you can: This will help the audience feel connected to you.

Use open gestures: This communicates honesty and certainty. Vary these gestures throughout the presentation to hold the audience's attention.

Direct attention: Point at the screen or walk closer to the audience to emphasise a point.

Be attentive: If there is an opportunity for questions, continue with your positive approach. Nod to show interest as the question is asked. Start by thanking the questioner and repeating the question to make sure you have heard correctly. Answer to the best of your knowledge and as succinctly as you can.

Look your best: Take some time with your appearance so you feel confident and professional.

Dealing with nerves

Presentation is 90% preparation, so plan, plan, plan and practise, practise, practise!

A well-planned, practised presentation will always go well. If you can, pause before you start your delivery, make eye contact and smile. This small space will give you a moment of calm so that you can adjust to being at the centre of attention. Good preparation will quickly kick in.

Strategies for staying calm:

- Prepare positively, set realistic goals and consider your material interesting and meaningful.
- Bring notes to help prompt you.
- Write down (and practise) neat transitions between slides.
- Work on an engaging and effective opening.
- Learn a few key phrases.
- Accept that you will be nervous and use the energy effectively.
- Visualise your audience as a supportive, interested group.
- Ask a friend to smile and nod, and look at them frequently.
- Breathe deeply and slowly.
- Speak slowly and precisely.
- Pause for emphasis.
- Sip water to prevent your mouth from becoming too dry.
- Remember the big picture. The world will keep turning; this presentation will soon be over.

Making presentations in a second language

Making presentations in your second (or third) language is an additional challenge. It is important to appreciate that the purpose of the presentation is to communicate your work to the audience, not to speak perfectly in the required language. Reciting flawlessly or reading directly from a script is less engaging than an imperfect language spoken more naturally, directly to the audience. Focus on the connection you make with them through your eye contact and gestures. This will draw them in and help them to listen more effectively.

Use your slides to support delivery.

Tips for presentations in your second language

▶ Speak slowly.
▶ Repeat important terms.
▶ Use simple language.
▶ Use relevant standard data measurements.
▶ Display key terms on slides, either as visual or as text.
▶ Use pictures.
▶ Present 'difficult' words on the slides.

Group presentations

Planning is crucial for a successful group presentation:

1 **Who is going to speak, when?** Decide from the outset. Allocate the same amount of time to each speaker.
2 **How are the slides to be prepared?** An effective method for labour division is to allocate each member of the group a certain number of slides.
3 **What is the slide format?** Use a standard template to prevent the presentation from appearing as a set of individual presentations.

Prepare your presentation well in advance of the delivery date. Each group member must be familiar with the entire presentation. Make sure you:

▶ Introduce each member of the group at the start of the presentation.
▶ Incorporate transitions between slides and speakers, for example, *'In the next slides Peter will explain the geology of the area.'*
▶ Pay attention to each other. Nod and smile while another member of the group is speaking. Show interest in the presentation.
▶ Know how to manage the slide transitions. Are you going to pass round a clicker? Will one member manage this? Do not decide this during the presentation!
▶ End with a final, conclusive slide.

On the day

Dress and conduct yourself in a professional manner. Bring enough handouts for everyone, if required. Do not overrun. If you find you are running out of time and still have slides to get through, refer people to the handouts, summarise the main points and move to the concluding slide.

Workshop 14: Group inventory

Complete the table.

	Preparation (name)	Speaker (name)	Time allocated
Title			
Introduction			
First point			
Second point			
Third point			
Conclusion			

Once you receive the mark for your presentation, work through Part 4 to reflect on your feedback and improve on your performance in future assessments ...

Part 4 is about **reflecting** on your performance, mark and feedback, and about **improving** for next time.

To improve your performance on assessments you first need to reflect on areas you most need to improve in. Your tutors give you clear indications in their feedback. But how often do you (honestly!) read and act on that feedback?

To improve

Feedback   Be the best you can

REFLECTING

Looking ahead

- Formative assignments are extremely valuable – use them well!
- Always read your feedback. Understanding and acting on feedback points is the quickest and easiest way to improve your performance (marks, ability to impress others, landing your dream job) in the future.
- If you do not agree with feedback or understand it, ask your tutor to explain.
- Compare feedback with that of fellow students or previous feedback you have had for a poster or presentation. Are there common themes? What one thing could you work on for improving next time? Can you suggest improvements to each other?
- Feedback is good!
  - Tutors who write lots of comments on your work are taking time to help you improve your performance.
  - Tutors are more likely to write lots of comments when they expect these to be read and acted on. Make the most of it!
  - Tutors' comments are not personal or a reflection of who you are but are intended to help you improve the quality of your work.

Common mistakes students make. These thoughts will hold you back:

Formative assessments are a waste of time— they don't even count towards the final mark!

I never read the feedback – I can't read my tutor's handwriting anyway.

Once I've got my mark there's no point in thinking how to make it better – the mark won't change.

The harder I work (and the better my mark gets!), the more comments my tutor makes on my work – it's demoralising!

Once I have handed in a piece of work I can forget about it. Only the mark counts in the end.

My tutor writes so much on my work, it makes me feel like there is no hope.

Formative assessments are designed to give you **feedback on how to improve**. Staff use these to train you in skills for later assignments, identify your strengths and weaknesses and guide you to the resources you need to improve your performance for next time (when it *will* count towards your final mark). Staff will also use your performance on formative assessments to gauge your professional attitude towards your work when writing references for you in the future.

Feedback, feedback, feedback

Feedback serves a number of purposes. It:

▶ lets you know what you are doing right
▶ highlights areas for improvement
▶ tells (and shows) you how to improve
▶ directs you to helpful resources.

Write a plan to follow for your next assignment

Identify main areas for improvement

Relate feedback and marks to assignment guidelines and assessment criteria

Read feedback comments

Feedback from students

Posters and presentations are visual assessments that are usually shared amongst the group. Make sure you look at the other students' work and identify strategies you could use next time. Talk to your friends and other students. What did they think of your poster or of your presentation?

Some poster and presentation assessments involve **peer review**. Students read/listen to and evaluate fellow students' work. This is an extremely valuable exercise. By thinking critically about others' posters and presentations (what they did well, what they didn't, what you understood, what you found confusing), you will learn to re-evaluate your own work with a more objective and self-critical eye. The euphoria of completing an assignment can lead to a distorted sense of how good it is. Having seen what fellow students did, you may identify a host of mistakes as well as good points in your own work that you simply didn't notice before. Make a note of these and create a reflection sheet for next time.

Workshop 15: Reflecting to improve

→ Gather your poster or presentation slides, assignment instructions, assessment criteria, feedback sheet and notes from the workshops in this book. If you filmed your presentation, watch the video again.
→ List your main feedback points. From these, identify your strengths and weaknesses.
→ Follow the flow diagram on the right.
→ For each point, write down a list of actions to help you improve in the future.

Feedback you received – and actions to improve. Revisit these workshops:

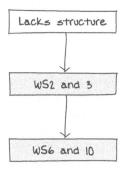

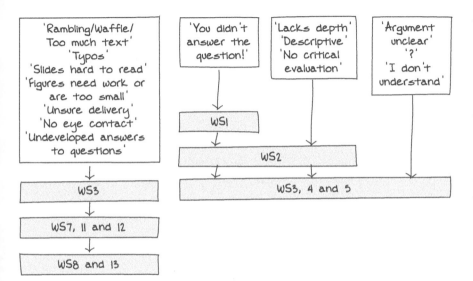

Most universities have student support services that offer additional training for students. Topics will include writing skills, literature searching, critical evaluation skills, mathematical and statistical skills, time management, public speaking. Use these resources. They are free at the point of the use and will greatly improve your performance.

13 Looking ahead

In this book we have shown you how to make persuasive posters and presentations for university assessment at undergraduate level. But let's step back and take a look at the bigger picture: applying your skills in the real world.

Whether for professional or personal use, being able to present yourself effectively will always be of value to you. The next step after university may be further study or looking for a job. In both cases your poster and presentation skills will be needed.

Higher education

If you stay on at university to do a Masters degree or PhD, you will probably give an oral presentation or present a poster at a departmental seminar or academic conference. The workshops in this book may be useful for getting you started on these.

At postgraduate level the emphasis moves from demonstrating learning to communicating new knowledge. You will need to identify the most interesting findings or outcomes from your work, and find an appropriate angle for your academic audience.

Conference tips

In general:

▶ Take business cards or contact information.

▶ Always include logos of all funders and supporters of your work.

▶ Use the official university slide template if you have one.

▶ Try to speak to people in person – they are more likely to remember you.

▶ Remember, first impressions count: dress well, act professionally at all times.

▶ Prepare a one-minute synopsis of your poster or presentation: consider it as an opportunity to give a guided tour of your work.

▶ Do not be disheartened if you feel you are not getting much attention. It takes time to develop networking skills. And remember, it only takes one future supervisor or employer to take note of you and your work for it to be a success.

▶ Consider each person you talk to as a potential future employer or supervisor and speak to them with this in mind.

▶ Check if your university or learned societies offer travel funds for students to attend.

Posters

- Make it visually appealing: you have seconds to grab attention amongst intense competition.
- Make it interesting: people spend less than 5 minutes viewing a single poster (Berg 2005), so make yours count.
- Have plenty of A4 handouts available.
- Be by your poster during scheduled poster sessions.
- If allowed by the conference organisers, you may want to try providing Post-it® notes which people can stick on your poster to provide comments and feedback.
- If you are flying to a conference abroad, are there flight restrictions on cabin baggage dimensions? If you need to transport your poster with the checked baggage you will need a durable tube.
- After the conference display, your poster will be exhibited on a wall at the university. It will reinforce your contribution to the department and inform visitors and new students and staff of your research field and findings.

Presentations

- Ensure your message is clear and relevant: you need to hold your audience's attention.
- Use the question time at the end as an opportunity to test ideas and get feedback from the (often expert!) audience.
- Be available to talk to people after your presentation slot: this is when people will come to find you.

In the workplace

Your presentation and communication skills will be crucial both for landing your dream job, and thriving and progressing once you have it. Try doing Workshop 16 on the following page.

No matter what sort of environment you aspire to work in, they will all require you to work alongside and communicate effectively with other people. These may be family, work colleagues, members of the public, business competitors, the media. In all cases, effective visual and spoken communication skills are key to getting a toe in the door, and then climbing the career ladder once you are in. Don't forget that however far you go in your chosen profession, you will always need to reflect on your performance so you can continue to improve and be the best you can.

Workshop 16: Applying your skills in the real world

My dream job is: ....

My poster and presentation skills are useful to this role in the following ways:

Example 1: What? *Interview*
                 How? *First impressions – smart, professional, good communicator, enthusiastic, knowledgeable*

Example 2: What? *Team meetings/interacting with the public*
                 How? *Work effectively in a group, communication (including listening) skills, communicating with individuals from different educational and cultural backgrounds*

Your example 1: What? ....
                       How? ....

Your example 2: What? ....
                       How? ....

Whether at university, work or play, enjoy using your newly honed visual and verbal communication skills to connect with people, share ideas, and make a difference in all areas of your life!

References

Berg JA (2005). Creating a professional poster presentation: focus on nurse practitioners. *Journal of the American Academy of Nurse Practitioners*. 17, pp245–8.

Christenbery TL and Latham TG (2013). Creating effective scholarly posters: a guide for DNP students. *Journal of the American Association of Nurse Practitioners*. 25, pp16–23.

Miracle VA (2003). How to do an effective poster in the workplace. *Dimensions of Critical Care Nursing*. 22(4), pp171–2.

Rowe N and Ilic D (2009). What impact do posters have on academic knowledge transfer? A pilot survey on author attitudes and experiences. *BMC Medical Education*. 9, p71.

Rust C, Price M and O'Donovan B (2003). Improving students' learning by developing their understanding of assessment criteria and processes. *Assessment & Evaluation in Higher Education*. 28(2), pp147–64.

Science (2013). Posters & graphics. *Science*. 339(6119), pp514–15. http://www.sciencemag.org/content/339/6119/514.full.pdf.

Shin SJ (2013). Evaluation of electronic versus traditional format poster presentations. *Medical Education*. 46(5), pp519–20.

Trimble V (2010). Posters from the edge of the universe. *New Astronomy Reviews*. 54, pp178–80.